Recollections of the Plymstock Area

Dorothy Warley Pitt

Four Views of the Area
Postcards frequently show local scenes and they have been a great source of local records, especially the very early ones. This card dates from the 1950s and shows changes even over the past few decades.

This version of the book is virtually as originally published, presenting the work of Dorothy Warley Pitt. There are now additional pages at the back providing information about the publisher, Arthur L Clamp.

The republishing project is being managed by Arthur's grandson, Steven Gibson. We aim to find all the research that he was involved in publishing, preserving it for the next generation as part of 'The Clamp Collection'.

PLYMSTOCK OF OLD

When Plymstock was a pretty village
Trees and fields instead of houses
Horse and cart instead of lorry
No one ever in a hurry
In Plymstock of old.

When my late mother was a young girl, she came to Plymstock from her native village of Holbeton in order to work here. The names of her employers were Mrs. Clarke, a retired Army officer's widow, and Commander Jones, who was Mrs. Clarke's brother. Their house, which was called Russell House, stood at the top of what was then known as Vicarage Hill, but is now Church Road. It has long since been demolished and a new estate built on it, but there are still a few of the older folk in Plymstock who remember it, situated just opposite Cooke's Farm. She told me that at that time there were only a very few houses between Plymstock and Oreston, and the only transport was the steamer for Plymouth. Almost the first thing she noticed was that although there were plenty of hedgerows, primroses did not grow there as they did at Holbeton and Yealmpton, but there were a few white violets.

I was told that Mrs. Clarke's husband caught a chill through sitting out on the lawn of his home after returning from a hot climate, and he died soon afterwards while still young. Mrs. Clarke always carried his photograph with her if she went away to stay anywhere. There were three young nieces who used to visit them at Russell House. One lived on at Plymstock for many years, but the other two went away and kept a boarding house in another part of the country. I don't think any of them married. My mother lived there from 1899 until 1901, when she left to marry my father, who was an Oreston man.

UP PLYMSTOCK, DOWN ORESTON

As I have mentioned before, there was a *thin red line* for many years between Plymstock and the surrounding villages, but, of course, with the ever increasing population this has died out over the years. I think, regarding old Oreston, which was a seafaring village at that time, it was brought about not so much by the inhabitants, but by the many foreign sailors who came there in little ships and *got drunk* in one of the several public houses which were in the village then. So I think that was why the Plymstock folk kept largely to themselves. Mrs. Clarke did not think much of anyone marrying an Oreston man. One day she saw a woman pass by with a bright red hat on, and noticed her because very few came that way in those days. So she remarked, "I don't know that person. I think she must have come up from Oreston," meaning by the way she was dressed.

There even seemed a different intonation when folk said, "Up Plymstock," and "Down Oreston." Anyway the village church folk of Oreston were permanently *Up Plymstock* at the last when they died and were buried in family graves.

WARREN'S CHARITY

The Warren Charity has been of great benefit to the parish of Plymstock over the years, particularly when people were very poor. Under the terms of a long-ago vicar, Rev. Vincent Warren, of St. Mary and All Saints Church, Plymstock, money is payable for clothing *poor children* between the ages of five to eight years. Nowadays the money is paid in the form of clothing vouchers. Years ago some parents would not allow their children to receive it because they had to wear certain rather ugly clothes which identified them as receiving the charity, and sometimes this made them feel humiliated.

I have heard another interesting fact regarding old Plymstock. A woman speaker addressing a recent meeting at one of the Women's Guilds in the parish said, during the course of her talk, that Plymstock, Goosewell and Staddiscombe were 900 years old, as recorded in the Doomsday Book.

BURROW LODGE

Some interesting information came to my knowledge a few years ago regarding old Plymstock houses, one of which is Burrow Lodge. After the Battle of Waterloo, Napoleon Bonaparte attempted to escape to America, but was apprehended at Rochefort where he surrendered to Captain Maitland, R.N. The dejected prisoner-of war was transported across the Channel in H.M.S. *Bellerophon* en route for St. Helena, transferring at Plymouth to H.M.S. *Northumberland* for the final stage of the journey. Some years later on being found unseaworthy H.M.S. *Bellerophon* was moored in the Hamoaze as the convict ship *Captivity*.

When the historic ship was broken up in 1836, Sir Frederick Maitland bought the figure-head and stern ornaments, and amongst purchasers of the timber was George Bellamy, M.D., who was the ship's surgeon at the Battle of the Nile in 1798 when following an engagement with the *L'Orient*, the majority of the ship's company was killed or wounded. George Bellamy entered the Navy in 1793 as surgeon's mate on board H.M.S. *Myrmidon*, commanded by Lt. John Burrow, his maternal uncle.

Lt. Burrow died in 1818, his father, John Burrow, of Plymstock, in 1797. Their epitaph in St. Mary and All Saints Church, Plymstock, reads:
"Men who did justice, loved mercy,
and walked humbly with God".

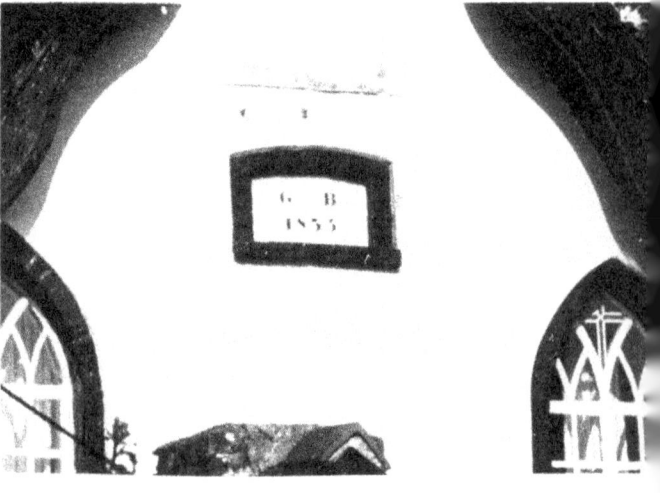

G B

The Church Road and Horn Lane houses (lower picture) link the area with the article about George Bellamy.

With his Bellerophon timber George Bellamy of George Street, Plymouth, built a cottage in the Gothic style at Plymstock where he had inherited land from his father and uncle. Cannon balls placed alongside the narrow, winding staircase were further reminders of the old ship.

MARCHANT HOUSE

Another interesting house in Plymstock was *Marchant House*, near the old Vicarage. At the time my mother was living in Russell House, the people who lived there were called Parsons. The father, the late Mr. Charles Parsons, was a master builder, and in his day he built several houses in the parish, including some at Hooe. He was a tall, smart man, but was bedridden for several years before he died. His wife was a cheery little white-haired woman, although she had had quite a lot of trouble. Before her marriage she lived at Calstock. They had a fairly large family of sons and daughters, but several of them died young, only Bessie and Meta were left in the end. None of them ever married, as their father had rather decided views of bringing them up, so they did not mix socially, but stayed in quite a lot and did embroidery.

Miss Bessie Parsons had a fuller life as she became a schoolteacher, and taught in her latter years at Goosewell School. When she was training or working in Plymouth her father used to meet her from the steamer at Oreston with a pony and trap, as it would have been a very lonely walk home to Plymstock on dark nights especially in those days. When the girls were at last free to mix socially they were too shy to go owing to their victorian upbringing.

They were kind to my mother when she lived nearby, and occasionally invited her to tea. She always kept in touch with the family, and visited them at intervals after she was married. Miss Bessie Parsons was the last survivor. I remember when as a schoolgirl my mother used to take me with her occasionally to visit them. Mrs. Parsons had a rather large, dark, living room, and she had several toby jugs with rather ugly faces on her dresser which I did not like looking at. She nursed her husband for years very patiently, and only lived a few months after him. I think they are all buried in the graveyard attached to Plymstock Parish Church, as they used to attend there, and people did not favour cremation in those days.

The late Mr. Jim Symons, of Church Road, Plymstock, told me that *Magnolia Cottage*, now demolished, which was near the surgery on the opposite side of the road, was one of the oldest cottages in Plymstock, but was of no historical interest, only a farm cottage. There is a new house there bearing the same name. *Peek's Cottage* was also considered to be the oldest remaining cottage. Mrs. Townsend's father, the late Mr. Lavers, built a cottage behind the *Plymstock Inn* and cottages either side, then he lived in one of them. He was the first landlord.

SOME LOCAL FARMS

Of the nearby farms, Court Farm, Dunstone Road, was a part of the glebe land of the church, and Downhorn Farm, Horn Lane, of Georgian architecture, was rumoured to have a secret passage leading from it to the church, which was said to have been used by the monks at the time of their persecution.

Plymstock School Prefects

Plymstock area has been served for many years by a very good school with many staff and young people who have earned high praise both from near and far. Many pupils leave this area for further education and the record of the school can bear favourable comparison with others of its size. Here a group of prefects stand for the camera sometime during the 1950s smartly attired and ready to face a challenging world when they leave the school for the last time.

ORESTON AND ITS FOLKS

One of the best loved curates in olden days of Plymstock Parish Church was the Rev. W. J. Ahier who was there during the 1914-18 War. He was in charge of the daughter Church of the Good Shepherd at Oreston, and has been long remembered by older folk for his kindness and generosity. He has been described as a "Real Christian" by the few left who still remember him. One of his good deeds was to take two hessian bags filled with gifts, which he used to take to those he considered needed them, attached to his bicycle. He did this quite often, paying for them out of his own money, when everyone was poorer than they are now, and food was difficult to get in wartime. He later left Oreston to become vicar of St. Mary's Parish Church, Brixton, but he corresponded regularly with the late Mr. William Lawson and his wife, and they visited him.

Later on he felt that he would like to become a missionary, as he was a bachelor with no close ties, so the Society for the Propagation of the Gospel decided to send him to work under the Bishop of St. John's, Kaffraria, who wanted a priest to take charge of a district (really two districts), called Maclear in Griqualand East; the work being chiefly among Europeans. So he left Brixton for South Africa about August, 1924, but still corresponded regularly with his friends at home. He died there.

Another popular curate, also in charge of the Church of the Good Shepherd long ago, was the Rev. W. Yates, who lived with his family in Endsleigh Road, Oreston. He lived to be over eighty.

Miss Baron was the organist at that time. She used to live at Prince Rock, and walked in from there with her mother and sisters. After her marriage, she was succeeded by Mrs. K. Lawson, who was an organist there for many years. Others who were deputy organists were the late Mrs. M. Stamp, the late Mrs. Primrose Bolt (my eldest sister), and Mrs. Mildred Pascho, the last named now living at Hooe.

I have been told that the Church was originally one large mission room, but the rest of the building was gradually added on. The present organist is Miss Joyce Tope, formerly of Oreston, and now living at Plymstock.

MRS. WILLIAMS

Touching on a humorous note, over ninety years ago, a Mrs. Williams, who lived nearby the church, used to ring the bell for Sunday services. The local lads nicknamed her "trousers". When I remarked, "Surely she didn't wear trousers or jeans, as in those days people would have been shocked", this was the explanation given to me. Apparently Mrs. Williams used to wear a long gown, as was the fashion then, but when she pulled the bell her frilled pantaloons showed underneath. Hence the nickname. About the same time there was a very popular lay reader. He was a Church Army man, named Mr. Marchant, and he also used to be very interested in youth work. Once a week, besides holding services at the church, he used to gather the boys together on the Quay in what was described as a "glorified washhouse" and talk to them in a very interesting way. Unfortunately, they did not always remember what he taught them, because very often on the way home they would go into Lizzie Passmore's corner shop, blow out the candles she kept lighted there, and run off with handfuls of her

By the way, I was told several years ago now, that Mr. W. H. Coleman was probably the longest serving chairman of the old Plymstock Parish Council. He was on the Parish Council for forty years and Chairman for about twenty five. There was only another one ever heard of who served as long, and his name was Coleman too, he lived in another county.

The Rev. W. J. Ahier

Many people will recall this once well known figure walking in the area. He held two morning services at the Church of the Good Shepherd, Oreston; 8 a.m. and 10 a.m., and he is here photographed in the vicarage garden.

Inscribed Stone in Wall

A careful search of the wall almost opposite Watts, the Florists at Oreston, should reveal this limestone block set in position with *I x Q 1797* cut into it. It would be very interesting to know the origin of this stone and how it came to be placed here. If anyone could give me information about it, I would be most thankful.

Plymstock Brownies

The hats almost give away the decade of this photo of the 1920s showing a meeting of the First Plymstock Brownies. Although names have not been found to match the young people shown, I am sure some will be recognised and the occasion may even be recalled.

Plymstock School Class

This class photograph was taken during the 1920s with the teacher standing on the left. In spite of many enquiries no names have come forward to identify the young people or the teacher. Perhaps someone will recognise one or two in this book.

Wartime Gardening

Great efforts were made in all areas during the First World War to till land and raise crops. Here boys, under the direction of the headmaster, are tending to a large garden specifically planted for food in 1917. This was at the back of the school.

Constable Payne and His Family

James Payne was transferred from the Exeter area to Plymstock in 1890 and was the local "Bobby" until his death in 1903. The police house still stands at the top of Stentaway Road and was formerly part of the much older workhouse. The upper picture shows him with his wife Annie with four of their seven children and the later picture below shows two sons in uniform, Frederick on the left and Reginald on either side of Cicely (Cis). Wilfrid is on his father's knee, then Evelyn, Charles and Harold and their mother (nee Page). Descendants of this family have lived in Burrow Farm for many years.

The Young People of the 1950s

Every decade brings its own faces and events in which many young people engage from sports to drama and entertainment. These two scenes come from 1952 (upper) and 1954. Speech day at Plymstock School in 1952 was marked by a display and physical training demonstration under Miss Hoare's supervision. Below the camera records smiles and enjoyment on the faces of members of the cast for *Jack and the Beanstalk* presented in December of that year. The cast is with Miss Budge and Mr. Ratcliffe.

The Church Tower of St. Mary's

This forms a centre point for the very rural scene captured in this pre-war photograph. Although not too much has changed around the church itself, the wider area would almost certainly be unrecognisable to people returning after thirty years or more. The view is taken from the slopes of Burrow Hill.

Relaxing with Tea

The Rev. Charles H. Wreford and his wife, Agnes, take a well earned rest in the vicarage garden following a full day's work. Mrs. Wreford undertook much voluntary work in this area and her husband was popular with the parishioners.

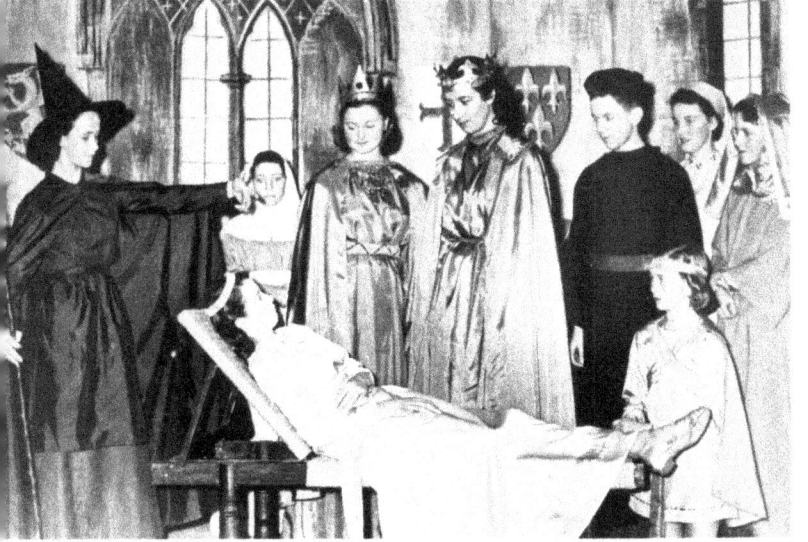

Local Productions

There has been a strong tradition in the Plymstock area, both in schools and societies, for plays to be staged in the school, village hall or in Plymouth. Here the case is photographed in 1952 in what looks like a *Joan of Arc* scene, but, to date, no details have been forthcoming about the people in it. No doubt some will be recognised by people still living in the area.

P.T. Enthusiasts

Some of Plymstock's young girls of the 1930s are assembled here at a display of physical training. Among them are Audrey Shillabeer, Doreen Crocker, Kathleen Reynolds, Winifred Harling, Diana Camp, Joan Truscott, Leonora Nurse and Margaret Tancock.

School Production

Mr. Ratcliffe was the driving force behind this school production of *Babes in the Wood* in 1952. Pupils of Plymstock School normally stage a special event for the Christmas period and the happy faces here reflect the pleasure gained in the production which was, no doubt, also enjoyed by the audiences which support these kinds of events.

OLD ORESTON AND ITS FOLKS

The men of old Oreston
Sailed with the tide
And some of their families
Went by their side.

We real Oreston folk love the sea. Say what you will, we have the sea in our blood, even in this modern day and age. Although we do not realise it until we go away, we are never really happy away from the sight of the water and the salt tang of the sea.

What can you expect, descended as we are from generations of seafaring folk. Yet the sea, which we love, has brought tragedy and bereavement time after time in days gone by to inhabitants of our village from one generation to another. Sometimes a man has been cut off in middle life while in a foreign port, many have died after reaching home through shock and exposure. Some have died very near home. My own grandfather, Elias Warley, a merchant seaman, died from typhoid fever which was probably aggravated by exposure, at the early age of twenty-five. Apparently he was home at the time as my father had not long been born, and took odd jobs, one of which was to fetch liquor round about Christmas time from the *Passage House Inn* just across the water, and bring it back to the *King's Arms*, at Oreston. He got caught in his rowing boat coming back on what was then, and still is, known as "The Nab", which is a spur of land between Oreston and Hooe which cannot be seen at high tide and had to wait until the tide rose again before he could get home.

My grandmother, who was only nineteen then, was left, without any pension and a baby son, my father. She was a wife, a mother and a widow in thirteen months, and remained a widow for sixty-nine years, until her death during World War two at the age of eighty-eight. When old age pensions finally came in, she and others had to wait until they were seventy before they could draw it, but even so they thought it was wonderful to have anything at all.

OLD ORESTON CAPTAINS AND BOATS

One of the old Oreston captains and their ships between 1870 and the early 1900 period was Captain Stephen Carder, of the *Bessie Simmons*, whose brothers often accompanied him, one of them being Captain Isaac Carder. Another brother Carder was drowned in another ship on a voyage to Newfoundland where they used to travel to buy fish. Then there was Captain John Tope, and also Captain Philip Ellis, who with his father, Captain Joseph Ellis, went to sea in a large smack called *The Providence*. My great-grandfather, Captain George Warley West, like the others, at one time had his own ship. His late grandson, Mr. George West, late of Hooe Villa, near the disused railway line facing Radford Lake, told me that great-grandfather's ship was called *The Fruiter*, probably because he carried fruit as a cargo quite often. It was a ketch. He was one of the first to take coal to France after the Franco-German War, and landed there not knowing at the time that the two countries were at war. He took three of his sons with him, and the youngest, Bill, who was the cook, was imprisoned by the Germans for one night, for having come ashore without a permit. Captain George Warley West came from Scotland, and sometimes wore a kilt, probably on Sundays, of which he was very proud. On one of his voyages from Oreston someone stole the ship's meat before they left and they had to return to port. His daughter, grandmother Ann Pillidge Warley, dreamed that the meat was hidden in the Oreston Quarry,

Captain Ernest C. Tope, Oreston

A very typical stand for many Oreston men who spent much of their lives at sea. Captain Tope was taken ill at sea and died in the Channel Islands in 1919 leaving a widow and two sons, Bill and Ernest.

where, sure enough, it was discovered in a well known cave there, but alas, "too late". Captain West suffered a severe stroke through worry as the result of this, and he died about twelve months after while still in his forties, and is buried in Plymstock parish churchyard.

By the way, granny said that in those days the *King's Arms* at Oreston used to have occasional parties, to which only the captains and their families were invited, and she could remember her father used to always buy her a new dress to wear on these occasions.

Other captains were Captain Bill Holten and Captain George Wyatt, of the schooner *Gertrude*. There was Captain Jack Johns, of the *Lewisham*, who, together with two sons, was lost at sea near Swansea during the Great War. One of the sons had been ill and went with him for a health cruise. They were buried near where they died. Bosun Henry Samuel Ellis died at Durban while with the Eastern Telegraph Company on 6th May, 1931, after he had caught a violent chill. He left a widow and two sons, and was only 52 at the time of his death. His widow, Mrs. Lily Ellis, lived for many years after his death. His brother, William Ellis, was drowned off Cornwall on the *Eve* the same year. A Mr. Peel, who came from Ramsgate with his wife and family to escape the bombing during the 1914–18 war lived in a cottage in what was then known as "Pump Street", Oreston, was also lost at sea off the Cornish coast. He was a fisherman. His wife, Mrs. Kate Peel, now deceased, told me that she

Church of the Good Shepherd Outing

This happy group of adults and children captures the enjoyment of the occasion when members of the Oreston church went on an outing in the late 1960s. Church outings and tea parties are still much appreciated and these people will easily recall happy times when members and friends came together for the day.

always left her door unlocked in the hope that he might one day return, but of course he never did. One son, Joe, still lives in the village. The cottage which was the family home is now demolished, as others.

Benjamin John Tope, when aged 56, was drowned on the *Ivy*, when travelling from London to Fowey in February, 1928. Captain Ernest Charles Tope was taken ill at sea and died in the Channel Islands in February, 1919. He left a widow and two sons. They took great risks at sea in those days, as there was no wireless and no motors in their little boats, and if in trouble at sea with no one near they often sank and were never heard of again.

I have had a conversation with the late Captain Ernest Charles Tope's younger son, Ernest, who is now 77, and an invalid, but very cheerful. He still lives in Oreston and can remember quite a lot about the village years ago. His elder brother, now dead, followed the sea like his father, but he told me his mother would not let him make it a career, although he had been with his father to St. Malo, France. He remembered taking over half a crown to Mr. W. H. Coleman, who was then a shopkeeper on the Quay, as payment for his father's boat being moored there. Mr. Coleman used to pass it on to the Duke of Bedford. Mr. Coleman, who was once piermaster of Morwellham Quay still has his name recorded at Morwellham.

OLD HOUSES AT ORESTON

Touching on some of the old houses, what was once known as Bayly's Farm, Oreston, but is now Holten House, has quite an interesting history. It was at one time the home of the Elfords, a well known Oreston family connected with the steamboats, and several of their ancestors were born there.

In the latter part of the last century it was a butcher's shop. Captain Charles Holten who lived there afterwards, was born on Oreston Quay, and died about the year 1934. He had a three-masted schooner called *The Elinor*, and went to sea when only nine years old. He went, among other places, to Spain, France, Holland and Belgium, taking with him on these voyages his wife, who was formerly Miss Mann, of Yealmpton, and their two daughters, Winifred and Margaret. Afterwards, on retiring after forty-two years at sea he came to Bayly's Farm and conducted a butchery and dairy business there from the year 1902. His youngest daughter, Mrs. Margaret Rapson and her husband carried on for some years afterwards with the dairy. The butchers at the farm before Mr. Holten were Mr. Wakeham and Mr. Elford.

The nearby Quick's Farm, afterwards known as *The Laurels*, and now the village post office, was farmed at different periods by the respective families of Edwards, Cooms and Bickfords. The late Mrs. Miriam Cooms first kept a dairy at Minnards House, Oreston. The *Forester's Arms*, "down yard", was once both a public house and a farm in the charge of Mr. Robert Bowden who owned fields then at Rollis Park, Lower Saltram, and other places. Milk and cream were very cheap then, and children would often go "down yard" for cream and eggs for breakfast at fabulous prices. Mr. Dean was the baker then, and he had a shop on the Quay. Mr. Dick Rudd was also a baker, there being two bakers in the village at that time. Mr. Williams was the butcher.

SEAFARING DETAILS

Touching again on the seafaring side of our village, I have a list of ships and their captains which two retired seafaring men took about a week to compile for me. They are both dead now. Of course, it is almost impossible to name all of them, but I can give you several which, if not recorded, may be lost forever.

Flower of Port Sole, schooner, Captain Bill Tope, *John Rees*, ketch, Captain H. Davis, *Thomas Edwin*, schooner,

Captain John Tope, *Fanny*, ketch, Captain Joe Ellis, *Plover*, ketch, Captain Joe Holten, *Susan*, ketch, Captain J. Tope and the *Advance*, a ketch.

My informant had been to sea in his younger days in the *Canterbury Belle* and the *Sultan*, both ketches, on the coast of London and Ireland, and had sailed across to France for potatoes and onions. *The Grace*, Captain Alfred Edward Kingwell, was wrecked at Teignmouth many years ago, and her figurehead was preserved and sent to the captain's wife, which their daughter had in her garden at one time.

Then there was a schooner called *The Rifleman*. Also two more old captains, Captain William Carder and Captain Stephen Carder. The former went to Salcombe, Charlestown and Falmouth and other places in a stone smack. *The Kathleen* travelled up and down the river with stone and coal, taking her last load on the day of the great blizzard in 1891. My great-grandfather, George Warley West, who hailed from Scotland, was the captain of a ship called *The Fruiter*, because it carried fruit to France and other places. I was told that he wore his kilt on Sundays if he was able. There was another Scotsman Mr. McOscrie who lived at Rame, Rollis Park, and he did the same. I thought at that time he was the first to do it here, but apparently he was not.

The *Alice* was a tug belonging to Bayly's Yard, Oreston, (afterwards known as Bayly and Bartlett), the only one they had. Captains were Captain Rogers, Captain Richard, Captain Sam Oxland, (who lived opposite what was then known as *Chievley Hall*). Captain George West, Captains Bill and Sid Carder and Captain George Warley. The *Alice* was broken up during World War Two.

> O folk of Old Oreston
> With loyal hearts and true;
> We, who follow after
> Pay our tribute to you;
> If we had the courage
> That you had in the past
> We surely will be able
> Every storm to surpass.

OLDEST ORESTON LADY

I must mention the oldest woman ever known who lived in Oreston, Mrs. Blanche Norsworthy, who was in her 106th year when she died. She was born at Pomphlett, but lived most of her long life in Oreston. She used to tell people that her secret for long life was hard work and no worries. In her earlier days she sang in Plymstock Parish Church, but her life was mainly devoted to her family. As a young woman she brought up her own brothers and sisters before she married.

She married a member of an old Pomphlett family, the late Mr. Robert Norsworthy, and the wedding took place at Plymstock Parish Church in 1902, Queen Victoria's chaplain officiating. They had a family of five sons and two daughters, some deceased, some still living in the district, including grandchildren and great-grandchildren.

OLDEST ORESTON MAN

The late Mr. Caleb Samuel Carder was probably the oldest man in the village. Born in Oreston, he lived to be 95. Married twice, he served in the Army in World War One, in France, and afterwards was employed in Messrs. F. J. Moore's quarry at Radford, until the age of 71, when he received a medal for fifty-one years service. He died in August, 1971, leaving children, grandchildren, great-grandchildren and a great-great-grandchild.

He was always interested in the Oreston Rovers Football Club, and was a keen supporter. At his funeral there were red and white flowers, tied with scarlet ribbon, which were the Rovers' colours.

BOBBY HAWKINS

I must mention Bobby Hawkins, who lived in Pump Street, and who was quite a character. He lived in a cottage opposite the village pump, long since gone, and drove away anyone whom he thought misused it. He was short and dark, and always wore a seaman's peaked cap. He was apparently a bachelor or a widower. He claimed to be a direct descendant of Sir John Hawkins, but had not enough evidence to prove this. I have been told that the Lord Morley who lived at Saltram House then used to visit Bobby every Saturday morning in his carriage, and that Bobby had a large photograph of him in his cottage. So there seemed to be some truth in Bobby's tale.

THE FERRYMAN

Uncle Ned Harper used to ply a ferry boat from Oreston Quay to Cattedown Beach and charge one half penny each way. When any Oreston person got married, even if there was only one of them a villager, he used to fly the Union Jack from the ferry all day. My own father was honoured in this manner, and he was very proud of it. The last man to ply this ferry was Sammy White.

MRS. L. M. M. BIRCH

Another old Oreston woman who had a very hard working life was Mrs. Louisa Mary Martin Birch, who was a widow for several years, which was in the days when there were no pensions. She used to walk all the way to Saltram House from Oreston in order to work in the laundry, and walked all the way back. She had three sons, Manly and Charles

At The Park, Oreston

Mr. and Mrs. George and Lydia Warley pose for the photographer sometime in the 1930s.

survived to a fairly good old age, but the other died at the age of twenty-one. When she was older she kept a sweetshop for several years on the hill leading to the Church of the Good Shepherd. She lived to be seventy-nine, in spite of her hard life, and is buried in Plymstock churchyard.

Her son Manly had a very adventurous career. He joined the Army, and served in the Boer War and the South African War, and was given several medals. In the latter war he wore the uniform, which included a pill-box hat. He had a wonderful reception from the villagers when he returned from that war. That was when the village was small and most people were related to each other, which gave it a family aspect. He was a Gunner in the R.G.A. in the Boer War, and a sergeant in Salonica in the Great War, when he lost his wife. He had two daughters, Dorothy, now deceased, and Louie, and several sons. His younger daughter, now a widow, and one of her brothers still live in Oreston. Mr. Manly Birch rowed a boat from Oreston to the River Yealm with Caleb Carder for five shillings, and walked home. His brother, Mr. Charles Birch was employed for many years with the Plymouth and Oreston Timber Company, now Messrs. Bayly and Bartlett, and lived in one of their cottages in his latter years. He married a Turnchapel woman who lived many years after him, and had two daughters, Winnie and Edith and two sons, Charles and eldest son George. Charles is now dead but his widow still lives in Oreston, and George lives in Scotland, but his youngest daughter lives at Hooe, and the elder at Paignton. His wife Annie lived many years after him. Manly's brother Charles, also has a grandson and great grandsons living in Oreston.

Elias Warley of Oreston

He was one of the many Oreston men who was a merchant seaman. He died quite young leaving a widow and infant son, George Henry, aged four months.

FOREMAN'S HOUSE

The large house at the end of the Park drive, just outside the yard, was occupied for years by the respective foremen. When we were young it was Mr. Start, another was a Mr. Lewarn, whose daughter taught at Oreston School. This house stands high on a slope and commands a wonderful view of Hooe, Turnchapel and Plymouth and the surrounding district. It has had various names, which included *Kyan Cottage* and *Park House*. At one time years ago two families lived there, but I was told that they quarrelled because one of the tenants was a pianist and disturbed the other tenant too often. The Plymouth and Oreston Timber Company decided that from that time on there should only be one tenant. The house is still occupied, but the foreman no longer lives there, having chosen a smaller, more modern residence. Bungalows have been built on the site where the allotments used to be, opposite where the cottages were, and in front of what we called "The Plantation".

MR. JOE ALGATE

Mr. Joe Algate, who lived with his wife, daughter, her husband and young son Clarence, at Park Cottage, at the other end of our little private road, just inside the brown gate, used to keep the road in perfect order, cutting the hedges regularly. The other three tenants in the cottages adjoining ours when we were growing up, were Mr. Frank Start, only son of the foreman, and his family, Mr. and Mrs. Jim Carder and their three sons, and Mrs. Eliza Edwards. She had been a widow twice, her first husband being a Mr. Charlick from Hooe or Turnchapel, and her second husband a Mr. Edwards from Elburton. She had a son by both of the marriages and one grandson, Arthur. Mrs. Edwards took in washing and ironing, which she did very well, every day except Friday nights when she delivered her work around the village, and Sundays when she regularly attended the nearby Church of the Good Shepherd. My father was the captain of the *Alice* then, and Mr. Jim Carder was the stoker. Mr. Jack Ashford, who, I understood was a retired boat builder for Bayly's, lived behind Park Cottage.

TWO COBBLERS

There were two cobblers in Oreston then, the late Mr. Doddridge, who lived down *Turnquay*, and Mr. Fred Edwards who lived *Down Yard*, and both of them were cripples. Fred was very fond of pictures, and when I went to fetch shoes which he had repaired I was fascinated by the number of little pictures with which he had decorated his little workshop. Among the village dressmakers were the then Miss Lilian Doddridge, one of Mr. Doddridge's daughters, and Mrs. Beatrice Edwards, who came up from Cornwall when a young girl, and lived with her relations who kept a small general shop at *Gutter End*. She was much in demand in later years at Oreston carnival time as she was clever at making coloured paper dresses for children entering the fancy dress competitions.

There was a pretty lane just before you entered Park gate on the left hand side leading uphill and downhill to Radford, and over the wall was a fairly large orchard belonging to the late Mr. and Mrs. Charles Holten. The lane is a shambles now, and the orchard is full of houses, a few private ones, and council houses, aptly named *Orchard Crescent*. Up the lane and over the stile there was a little rough piece of land which we children loved to play in, the girls climbing the tree by the wall and the boys sometimes camping out there on summer nights. We always regarded it as ours, but alas, it was eventually sold and a bungalow built on it.

Oreston has not got, like several of the nearby villages, a hall for general use of the public. My old employer, the late Mr. E. A. Roberts, free-lance journalist, of Oreston, told me he once offered to buy a piece of land there which would have been suitable for such a communal building, but he could not get anyone to help in this project.

By the way, I have been told that long ago there was a shed attached to the wall "Down Yard" outside Bayly's, where emigrants used to sleep the night before they sailed for foreign lands. There used to be a wooden form there too, at one time.

LOCAL SCHOOLS

At this period the Pomphlett girls used to have to attend Oreston Primary School as well as the Oreston girls. Head mistress was Miss Culiss, another teacher being Miss Lewarne. The boys had to attend Dean School, Plymstock, my father being one of them. If the girls at the Oreston School were clever enough they were made pupil teachers, and Mrs. Watts was made one of those, the other being the late Mrs. Elsie Kingwell, of Oreston, who in later years taught me when I was in the infants' class. Mrs. Kingwell, as shown, continued teaching as a career after she was married, but Mrs. Watts had three daughters, and spent several years in Canada with her husband and family. She told me that she would have liked to have stayed there. Mrs. Kingwell had no children.

Another incident of rivalry between the villages was told to me by an old Plymstock man. His family house was about midway between Oreston and Plympton, quite near Plymstock School. As a young man he went courting at Oreston, but like others was driven away by the Oreston boys who wanted the girls for themselves. So he went the other way to Plympton, where he apparently was received more politely, and he eventually met and married a Plympton girl.

Three of Pearce's cottages, as they were then known, faced towards Pomphlett Lake, and were occupied at one time by Granny Maunder, her widower son John, and his sons, Bill and Ernest, who went to the old Dean School, Mr. and Mrs. Gotham, and Mr. and Mrs. Paige.

CAPTAIN ALF TOPE

Captain Alf Tope with his family, was on a ship called the *Carmenta*, a three-masted schooner. He travelled during his seafaring career to Belgium, north coast of Cornwall, Antwerp, Southampton, Poole and Dorset, carrying coal and clay. Mr. Jack Birch was the cook and Alf Brown the mate. These were two Oreston men, and there were also other members of the crew. Captain Alf Tope was described as a good man by one of his crew. He did not drink, listened to the church service on the wireless every morning, but did not force any of his crew to attend it. He always kept a good table, and was one of the most popular sea captains at that time. His brother Jack was on the *Ivy*, and travelled to the Gold Coast and Penryn, Cornwall. Captain Bill Wyatt also went to sea with his father, and brother Joe to Newfoundland for dry fish in small craft. Jack Tope on the *Ivy* lost his life at sea, leaving a widow, a son and a daughter.

THE HOOPERS

The Hoopers were a family who have long been remembered by Oreston folk. Mr. George Hooper (known as Harry Hooper) lived at 6, Park Cottages, Oreston, in the late 1800s. His wife survived him, and left that cottage about 1909. They were a strong Methodist family, and regularly attended Oreston Methodist Church. Mr. Hooper was employed in what was then called *Bayly's Yard*, or the Plymouth and Oreston Timber Company, for many years. It is now known as Bayly and Bartlett.

Mr. Hooper was a big, strong man, and he was very well liked. His sons were very clever. Herbert Hooper, next to the youngest child, passed twenty-third on the list of apprentices in all England when he qualified for the Dockyard. One son was in the Customs, and another, William, became a doctor. There were also daughters.

"THE PARK"

Their little cottage, now demolished, was very dear to me, as my brothers and I were born there and it was my home until I was about fifteen years of age. We always called it "The Park", Oreston, on our letters. I still remember seeing the initials "G.H." carved on the back window sill and asking whose they were. "The Park" was very pretty then when we were growing up and probably years before our time, as it had pink and white hawthorn trees planted alternately up and down the little private road, and in May, when they were in blossom, it was a very attractive sight.

Class at Oreston

Mrs. E. Kingwell and Miss Lewarn were at the school during the 1920s. In this class are Arthur Hendy, Joyce Phillips, Doreen Kendall, John Norsworthy, Gordon Avery, Winnie Box, Stephen Weston, Fred Carter, Doris Passmore with many others.

Our little cottages were four together in a row. A large sycamore tree rather darkened the cottage next to ours where Mrs. Eliza Edwards, a widow, lived as it grew at the top of her little garden plot in front of the house. It was reputed that it had been planted by one of the captains of Bayly's tug, the *Alice*, in order to prevent people padding by from looking in. Not that many folk went by in those days, one would have thought he would have been glad to see somebody. This captain was called Mr. Rogers. Other bygone captains of the *Alice*, which was broken up during World War Two, were Captain Rickard, Captain Sam Oxland (who lived opposite Chievley Hall), Captain George West, Captains Bill and Sid Carder, whom I think, were brothers, and my father, Captain George Warley.

Radford House

The "Great" house of this area was Radford House which stood just to the north of what is now Radford Dip. The Bulteel family owned it until the collapse of the Naval Bank in Plymouth in 1914. It was then purchased with a large estate by the Mitchell family who disposed of the land and had the house demolished over two years, 1935 to 37. The Duke of Bedford's crest and date of the building shows the ownership of the hall in Oreston. Many buildings in Plymstock also have this mark of ownership on them.

Rogation Sunday

The Rev. Robert Ball is here blessing the crops in Mr. Camp's beanfield accompanied with choristers and friends from St. Mary's. This annual event was on the fifth Sunday after Easter and among those here recognised are Michael Payne, Frank Crowe, Ivor Treeby, Charles Payne and Arthur Cannford.

Changes of Recent Years

The face of Plymstock has changed completely since the 1950s when many developments took place and old roads were widened, some buildings were demolished and shops built. Horn Lane is seen on the left as viewed from the chemist's shop and Dean Hill widening was recorded in the lower view when many front gardens were being cleared for road widening. The changes of the past few decades were so common that often they were not recorded.

Fancy Dress Competition

Part of the Oreston carnival was the well-supported fancy dress competition. One occasion in the 1940s is seen here with Mrs. E. Holland, Mrs. D. Pitt, Mrs. E. Catling, Mrs. Short and her daughter Maureen, with Mr. Wilfred Glinn and Mrs. E. Williams and others.

TALES OF OLD POMPHLETT

*"Half sailors and half quarrymen
Were our old time Pomphlett men."*

As my little poem says, some of the Pomphlett men went to sea, but a large proportion worked in the nearby quarries. Oreston was the main seafaring village. Although they were so near to each other, each had rather a different way of life in those days. Big ships used to come up Pomphlett Lake, nearly the width of the Mill, carrying grain and coal from foreign parts. Mr. Sparrow was the owner of Pomphlett Quarry (Ben and Lewis). On the nearby bank, opposite the lake, lived Mr. Jack Battershell and his wife, Mr. and Mrs. Axworthy, Mr. Josiah Bateman and Mrs. Sam Bunker. All the men were employed in the quarry. Several people have been drowned in Pomphlett Lake, and there is an headstone on the right-hand side as you enter Plymstock Church in memory of one of them. I daresay several more were buried there who suffered the same fate, but they lie in unmarked graves as many people could not afford to buy gravestones in those days.

WESLEY CHAPEL

The chapel about that time was at the top of New Hill. It was called *Wesley Chapel* and afterwards became *Wesley Cottage*. A Mr. Mumford and his family lived there years afterwards. A Mr. Walters used to walk over from Plymouth in order to preach there and Mr. Thorning and his wife, from Oreston, used to assist. There was also a *Blue Ribbon Temperance Party*, which a farmer, called Mr. Sparks, assisted in conducting. He used to arrive in a pony and trap. Once he burned spirit at a meeting in order to illustrate his subject!

Mr. Lang (nicknamed *Obadiah* for some strange reason) kept the *Morley Arms* and coal store about the year 1884. He was fairly tall and stout in appearance. Married twice, he was a churchwarden at St. Mary and All Saints Church, Plymstock, and gave a bell. He is buried in the churchyard with his wife Maria, who died before him.

Abraham Hall was another old Pomphlett character. A cripple, nicknamed *Abal* (they appeared to be very fond of nicknames in those days), he worked in the Breakwater Quarry for many years, and was one of those who lost money when the Naval Bank broke in 1914. He had a sister called Mrs. Newton who looked after him very well. She lived not far away at Blackberry Lane which is now known as Pleasure Hill.

POMPHLETT MILL

The Mill at this time belonged to Mr. William Mitchell and was worked by a water wheel. At the back there was a shippen where he kept cows. His mother was the dairy maid. Millway Terrace and Millway Place, as they were known then, were built by Mr. William Mitchell and his brother Sidney, of Pomphlett Mill.

There were several interesting personalities in the village in those days, when neighbours helped each other and seemed like one big happy family. Nicknames were common, some were very apt, and they were passed down from generation to generation and still are. There seemed to be a certain amount of rivalry among the different villages, and they liked to keep what belonged to them to share amongst themselves. For instance, the late Mrs. Watts, who lived to a good old age, told me that about the year 1900, when she was a child, there was no drinking water, before the coming of Plympton water.

FETCHING DRINKING WATER

She and her friends used to fetch water from the Oreston pump, if possible, but I am afraid they were not always welcomed there by those villagers who wanted the water for themselves. So the adults and children used to trot back to Hine's Farm, Billacombe, with a yoke across their shoulders on which to hang the two buckets. After a while water was brought around in a barrel and you were allowed a couple of buckets full. When she was a school girl, besides helping to fetch water, which must have been very heavy to carry, she also used to take milk around every morning, for which she was paid the princely sum of twopence a week. I wonder what our modern misses would think of these jobs!

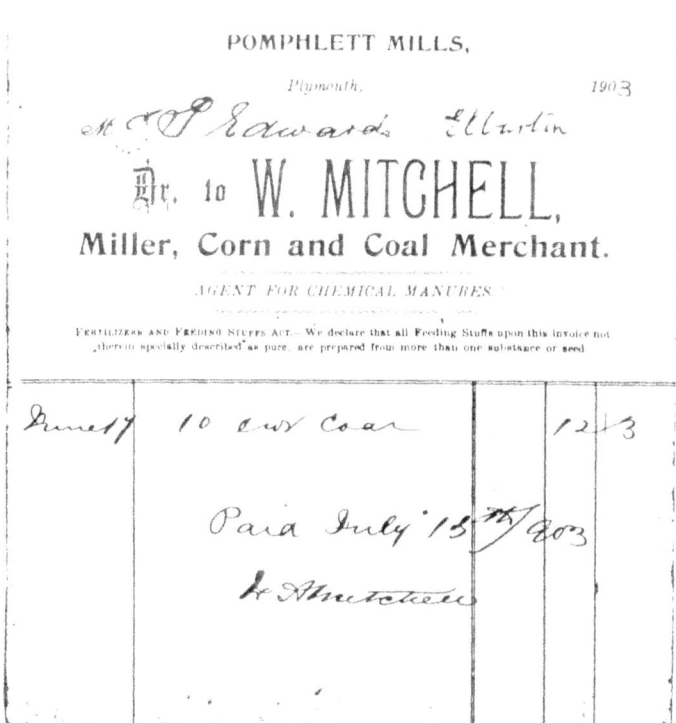

GRANNY MAUNDER

Granny Maunder was a little old woman who wore an old fashioned bonnet. She was one of the many widows who seemed to be around about this time, and we must remember that they had no pensions then. If their husbands died, probably through long hours and hard work, the women were just left to get on as best they could. So Granny Maunder, who seemed to be an independent person, earned a living by doing the village mangling with a very large mangle, for which she charged one half penny a piece, besides looking after her son and two grandsons. Other Pomphlett widows, as in other nearby villages took in washing, looking after mothers with newborn babies, scrubbed floors or took in sewing. They certainly did not have many idle moments in those far-off days.

Granny Maunder's neighbour, Mrs. Gotham, had a sister who was known as *Granny Gould*, who lived in the neighbouring village of Oreston, which at one time was only divided from Pomphlett by a little narrow lane. Their parents were called Beer and lived in what was then known as *Higher Pomphlett*, the district around the Mill being *Lower Pomphlett*. At Higher Pomphlett, when there was a wedding, they also had a way of honouring it as did Oreston folks. But instead of flying a Union Jack from the ferry all day as they did, they hung flags across the road between the cottages which must have been a pretty sight.

MUSICAL TALENTS

Of course, as I may have mentioned before, the men of Pomphlett loved music and singing and had nice voices. Mr. Carter was one who is still remembered. He was blinded by an explosion in a nearby quarry (Turnchapel) when about 30, but still played his musical instruments, at which he was very clever. Born in Elburton, he came to live at Pomphlett on his marriage to a Plympton woman, and spent the rest of his life there. Although he had never been taught, he could play the accordion, flute, mouth organ and whistle. He only played on one particular whistle, which had been picked up off the sea bottom by a diver. Every year the men of Pomphlett used to go on coach outings, when Mr. Carter used to take his brass whistle and his flute. They used to go to Chelson Meadow Races and to the Totnes Races. They had to save up all the year round for the Totnes trip, but they all thought it worthwhile, taking their concertinas and accordions and singing on their journey there and back.

> *Pomphlett, how it used to be;*
> *Now, though a different world I see*
> *There is a special place for me*
> *In the Book of Memory*
> *For old time Pomphlett.*

POMPHLETT, PLYMSTOCK,
SOUTH DEVON,

within a short distance of the Plymouth Boundary, close to Plymstock Joint Station on the Yealmpton Branch G.W.R. from Millbay and the L. & S.W.R. Turnchapel Branch from Friary, Plymouth.

To Merchants, Millers, Agricultural Co-operative Societies,
and all persons desirous of acquiring Waterside Mills and Stores.

PARTICULARS AND CONDITIONS OF SALE
OF AN EXCELLENTLY WELL-BUILT

Freehold Tide-Water Grist Mill
with DWELLING-HOUSE, COAL STORES,
and STABLING attached, known as

POMPHLETT MILLS
WHICH

MR. JOHN PEARSE

Has received instructions from the Owner, Mr. W. A. MITCHELL, to
SELL BY AUCTION,

At the Law Society's Chambers, Princess Square, Plymouth,
ON THURSDAY, 30th MARCH, 1922, AT 4-30 P.M.

Pomphlett Cottages

This very early picture shows part of the locality with the cottages and gardens butting onto the main road. Many changes have altered the place and some people may have difficulty in placing them in their present position.

Football Enthusiasts

Many football teams in this area have been supported by hundreds of children and young men. Here one team stands for the camera in the 1930s. The team is partly made up of Butler, West, McDonald, Johns, Steer, Body and two Carter brothers. No doubt the others will be recognised.

Radford House Lodge

Not much remains of this small building now but here it stands with Mrs. Repath by the large gate. She and John Repath lived there until 1955 and before them, Mr. and Mrs. Davis. The lodge was at the entrance of the long drive to Radford House and the various keepers were responsible for allowing people to enter and leave the one-time large estate.

The Breakwater Crew from Oreston

This renowned cutter and crew were famous in the area for their competitiveness in the boat races around Plymouth. Formed in 1903-4 the crew names were Isaac Passmore, Charlie Jackson, Bill Harper, Joe Jackson, Jack Dare, Jack Thorn, Sam Oxland, Jim Harper, Fred Rogers, Arthur Glinn, Joe Lugger, Bill Johns and Joe Brown.

BILLACOMBE.

Apter J J, 1 Boringdon terr
Fleming N, 7 Spencer terr
Fleming J, 6 Spencer terr
Gillard R, 2 Boringdon terr
Glasse Miss A, Billacombe vlls
Jackson J M, 8 Spencer terr
Leigh Mrs G, Billacombe vlls
Mitchell T H, Billacombe hse
Mundin C, 10 Spencer terr
Oxland L, 2 Spencer terr
Perraton J, 5 Spencer terr
Prigg H V, Billacombe vlls
Reeley F, Billacombe cotts
Soady W H, 1 Spencer ter
Stanlake G R, Billacombe vlls
Tresize M A, 12 Spencer terr
Williams S, 3 Spencer terr
Westlake J, 4 Spencer terr
Wyatt W, 11 Spencer terr

POMPHLETT.

Allen F C, Millway terr
Back G, Pearce's cotts
Bateman J, Morley's cotts
Birch E, Morley's cotts
Boulter S, The Cottage
Bright J, 5 Millway terr
Bunker E, Barn pk cotts
Bunker E E, Sunnyside
Bunker J jnr, Morley's cotts
Bunker R D, Coom's cotts
Bunker W, Scott's cotts
Bunker W S jnr, Coom's cotts
Bunker W J, Sunnyside
Burch J, 3 Staddon vw terr
Coad E, 1 Staddon vw terr
Congdon W H, Pearce's cotts
Couzins H, 2 Millway terr
Davis J, 2 Millway terr
Deacon J, 3 Millway pl
Down J, Coom's cotts
Evea P H, Sparrow's
Fall — 8 Millway terr
Goslin E, 1 Millway pl
Gotham F, Evea's cotts
Hackworthy S J, Coom's cotts
Hackworthy W, Scott's cotts
Hall A, Jacob's cotts

Hammett G,
Hendy E,
Hendy F H, Scott's
Hine J H, Pomphlett farm
Hockaday P, 6 Millway terr
House C, 3 Millway terr
Horn E, Evea's cotts
Horn S M, Evea's cotts
Jackson W, Coom's cotts
Jacob E, Pomphlett
Lowden R, 5 Staddon vw terr
Main T, Pearce's cotts
Marshall W H, 'Morley' arms
Mitchell S T, 12 Millway terr
Mitchell W A, The Mill
Mumford J F, Scott's cotts
Norsworthy R, Coom's cotts
Page W H, Evea's cotts
Pearse W, Coom's cotts
Peek J, 2 Millway pl
Pillage G, Blackberry lane
Pilliofe W, 7 Arundel vw terr
Pilliofe G, 8 Staddon vw terr
Revell R S, Coom's cotts
Revell T, Pearse's cotts
Revell W, Coom's cotts
Robert S, Blackberry lane

Skelly W, Evea's cotts
Thorne J, 2 Staddon vw terr
Thorne R, 4 Staddon vw terr
Thorning A, 6 Staddon vw terr
Voysey T, Pearse's cotts
West J, Barn pk cotts
West J jnr, Morley's cotts
Woods — 10 Millway terr

Local Directories

These gave lists of businesses and people and those shown here date from 1910. No doubt many of the names will be easily remembered.

TALES OF HOOE AND TURNCHAPEL

O little church upon the hill
In fancy I can see you still
And strange, wherever I may be
My thoughts so often fly to thee

I do not know much about the history of the Church of St. John the Evangelist, Hooe, but I have known several of the members of the congregation, including choirboys, who have travelled far away, and this is one verse of a poem which I have dedicated to them. It has been said that because of its situation between the two steep hills, as was thought to be fair to both villages sharing the church, one vicar left because of this.

HOOE CHURCH HALL AND OLD SCHOOL

At one time Hooe Church hall was used for some years as a schoolroom, before the present school came into existence down by the lake. One of the most popular headmasters was the late Mr. Edwin Rogers, who was also at one period master of Highweek Secondary School, Newton Abbot. He was at Hooe between 1922 and 1932, before moving to Highweek, until his retirement in 1956. He was a churchwarden at St. John's Church, Hooe, and also a churchwarden at Highweek Parish Church. He was well known in the town, and was a diocesan lay reader. On his retirement Mr. Rogers lived at Totnes, but still continued his Newton Abbot activities. A widower, he left one son, Paul, who was an actor. He died in a Torquay nursing home.

TURNCHAPEL SHIPYARD

The late Mr. Arthur Glinn, who last lived at Hooe House, gave me quite a lot of interesting information acquired during his long lifetime. One of the most well known and long lived inhabitants of Hooe and Turnchapel, he was born in the latter village at 7, Boringdon Terrace, but went to live at Hooe House in 1930, his wife, a Staddiscombe woman, dying eight years before him. He told me that the *Shipwright's Arms*, Turnchapel, got its name from the Turnchapel Yard, which at one time was the largest shipwrights yard outside the Dockyard. It was owned by a man called Pope, who probably built Mansion House, an interesting old building nearby. At one time there was a dry dock, and his mother could remember hearing the corking mallets. In Mr. Glinn's lifetime the Dock still existed but it was derelict. One of the cottages at the end of Turnchapel adjoining Mansion House was turned into a picture gallery by Mr. Pope in Mr. Glinn's mother's lifetime. Mr. Pope eventually went bankrupt, and the Naval Bank took over the Yard. At this time the Turnchapel steamboats used the foreshore for their landing, and the manager of the steamboats probably lived in Mansion House.

Tradition, according to Worth, has it that there was a small shipyard here at Turnchapel before the Dockyard was built, and it is almost certain that some of the ships which were used against the Spanish Armada were prepared and fitted out here. The Earl of Morley enclosed a dry dock there in 1797 and set out mooring chains for shipping.

Two 74's were built here in 1809; the *Armada* with a figurehead of Sir Francis Drake, launched in 1810, and the *Clarence*. They were launched with superb festivities, but their builder eventually went bankrupt. Later Turnchapel had a terminal station of a branch line of the Southern Railway, long since closed.

CIVIL WAR BATTLES

The village of Hooe has quite an interesting history, as has its neighbouring village of Turnchapel. In this short account I will try to relate some of this to my readers. It has seen its stormy days. Battles took place there in the months of October and November 1623, during the Civil War, when Plymouth supported Parliament, and, for a number of years, it was beseiged by the King's forces. Plymouth's most distant outpost was the one across the water on the heights above Hooe, which was Fort Stamford, now a country club, but in 1643 nothing much except earth works. From it soldiers could look down on the other side into Hawstart (now named Mount Batten after Captain Batten, a Parliamentary officer). The Castle was not built until some twenty years later, and it is reputed that some prisoners of war were buried under it. Mount Batten also overlooked Hooe, and beyond Hooe towards Plymstock, could be seen the Royalists headquarters at Radford.

ANOTHER HOOE

I thought readers would be interested to know that some years ago, while on holiday with my husband, I discovered another village named *Hooe*. It also had a very interesting history. While staying at Brighton, Sussex, we found it lying between Battle and Hastings, and there are now, or at the time we visited it, only two cottages left of the original village.

The reason for this, I was told, was that during the Great Plague of London a fourteen year old girl visited relatives at Hooe and brought the plague with her. Others said a traveller brought it in bales of material. As a result the whole village, with the exception of these two cottages, was burned down. The present Hooe village set in beautiful rural surroundings, is quite near the original site. It is said that smuggling took place there in bygone days, proof of which is a secret passage in the village inn which was used for that purpose.

There is a beautiful old church, dedicated to St. Oswald, the Rector of which at that time was the Rev. Henry C. N. Lawson, R.D. The sister church is at Ninefield, so the magazine was known as the *Ninefield and Hooe Magazine*. The two original cottages and the beautiful old church include some old ship's timber in their structure.

I was told that their interpretation of the word *Hooe* means a spur of land. I have heard of another. I have also heard that our village of Hooe sent two ships to the Spanish Armada. How far this was true, I cannot say.

Harking back to Hooe, near Sussex, an old Hooe lady, who has been dead several years now, said her brother discovered it when he was stationed near there in the Royal Navy. I have not met anyone who knew about it.

TURNCHAPEL YARD

Nearly eighty years ago the Shipwright's Yard was owned by a Mr. Kelly, who originally came from Yorkshire, but afterwards resided in Plymouth. Our late informant, Mr. Arthur James Glinn, who was over ninety when he died, was at that time a shipwright's apprentice there. He had to sign a seven years apprenticeship, and promise not to go into any public houses, and his wages were two shillings a week, with an increase of a shilling a year. His father had to provide his food and clothing.

At that period all the fields around Mount Batten were rented by a Mr. Hine of the *Castle Inn*, which was the only public house there, the only other houses being coastguard station residences. Fishing boats used to come from Lowestoft and other places, and they dried their nets in the fields.

OLD SHIPWRECK

About the year 1897 there was a wreck on the rocks off Mount Batten, at the time when Mr. Glinn was there. The ship wrecked was the hull of an old barque moored in the Sound and used for converting fish offal from the Barbican to fish manure. With others Mr. Glinn helped to drag the boat across the fields. The four pilots who rescued the crew were two Skilton brothers, Jack and Harry, Mr. T. Staddon and Mr. J. Pascoe. They all received a gold watch for their reward.

LOWER AND HIGHER SCHOOL, TURNCHAPEL

Mr. Glinn went to the school on Turnchapel Quay, which was then known as the Lower School, the teacher being Mrs. Jago, who afterwards became the head mistress of Oreston School. I can dimly remember her. She had one married daughter, Mrs. Bell, who lived with her in the adjoining school house at Oreston. She was a typical *School Mam*, with grey hair in a bun and glasses, and she was strict.

Goosewell School Group in 1929

How hard the children had worked for the concert! Doreen Crocker, Ewart Mutton, Audrey Shillabeer, Vera Lee, Doreen Reynolds, Kathleen Rich, Gladys Evans and Nesta Bight make up part of this group.

Higher School, to which the older children went, was at the top of the Lane where the building still stands, and children went there from the Lower School when they were about eight years old, just as later on the Oreston children went to Plymstock School. Mr. Glinn was a choirboy, and when there was a service they walked from the school to the nearby church. Rev. Tapson was the vicar then, and Mr. and Mrs. Walters were the school master and mistress. Choir boys were paid by the marks they received, and had one shilling for 100 attendances, and a steamer trip outing once a year to such places as Calstock. Mr. Morton, the organist of St. Andrew's Church, Plymouth, used to come over sometimes, more often on special occasions, and bring some of his choir, when there would be a musical afternoon, followed by tea.

HEXTON HILL SHOPS

At one time in the history of the village of Hooe there were several shops on Hexton Hill. Mr. and Mrs. Brent and Mr. and Mrs. Trott both had general shops there. Mr. Brent was nicknamed *Sacho*, for some unknown reason, and Mr. Trott was nicknamed *Gallop*, for obvious reasons, by the villagers. Mr. Harwood kept the bakery there. He had a daughter, Ruth, and a son named Alfred. His son-in-law succeeded him in the business. The butcher was Mr. Wakeham. Landlords of the *Royal Oak* at the foot of the hill have been Mr. Nat Pine and my late father-in-law, Mr. James Furse, who was once a sort of village doctor, as through his naval service he gained medical knowledge which he used to advise folk about their aches and pains. He was the first owner of the Hooe Social Club as it was then called.

Hooe Barton Farm, which was almost opposite the lake, was occupied about that time by two brothers, Mr. Ernest Sherrell and his brother George. Mr. Ernest Sherrell had two daughters named Dorothy and Edna. The former, who is now deceased, married Mr. Lew Benmore, whose father kept the *Victoria Inn* at that time. One of Mr. Pine's daughters married a Mr. Flanders, and afterwards people called Flanders kept the *Victoria Inn* also. Mrs. Kate Tucker also kept a general shop at Hexton Hill, and afterwards a shop at Turnchapel. She lived to a good old age, and had a very interesting and hard working life, of which I would like to tell you a little later on.

MRS. KATE TUCKER

Regarding Mrs. Kate Amelia Tucker, she lived a very long and useful life. She died in 1976 at the age of 92, leaving six daughters, 17 grandchildren and 19 great-grand-children. She first came to the city as a young girl, abandoned by her parents, and was sent to Plymouth from Cardiff Workhouse starting her Westcountry life in the Plymouth Industrial Home. At the age of fourteen she was sent out to service at Haye Farm, Plymstock, where she earned a monthly wage of one shilling.

She married a farm labourer and lived in and around Plymouth from then on. On her husband's early retirement she opened a small confectioner's shop at Hooe, later on taking over a general stores at Turnchapel, where she stayed for seven years. During both World Wars Mrs. Tucker did a great deal of voluntary work, particularly for the W.R.V.S. She was one of the two founder members of the Hooe and Turnchapel Sunshine Club and a founder member of the Turnchapel Ladies Football Club, as well as belonging to Hooe Mother's Union. She had kept in good healt, and died suddenly after a fall at her home. A funeral service, which was well attended, was held for her at St. John the Evangelist, Hooe, followed by cremation. She was said to be one of Plymouth's colourful and best known characters, and her daughter-in-law, Mrs. S. R. Tucker, said of her "She had so many interests in the city that you could write a book about her".

HOOE MANOR

An interesting old house in Hooe Manor, a Georgian squire's thirty-two room mansion set in ornamental gardens and thickly wooded grounds. It is listed by the Department of the Environment as grade two, with star, building and a fine ceiling, which are all credited to the Adam brothers. It was once the stately home of such famous local names as Harris and Bulteel, who also lived at Radford House. It is now let to council tenants.

There is a grand drive way flanked with a host of exotic flowers, and trees such as Japanese oaks and monkey trees. Tucked away in a quiet corner there is a lily pond stocked with fish. A magnificent central avenue leads from the front of the house to a balustrade-surrounded pool with statues which will spout a fountain when a pump and water are installed.

Hexton Wood Cave

The owner, Mr. W. A. Gordon Mitchell, is at the entrance to the cave watched by his son, Nigel. This was in 1952 when two young people were trapped.

MISS ALICE GREET

Miss Alice Greet was quite a character in her time. At the age of sixty-five she married an eighty year old mariner named Mr. William Skilton, a member of an old Turnchapel family. Before her marriage she had led a very quiet life, but she made up for it afterwards. She took up football as a hobby at the age of sixty-seven, and formed the *Turnchapel Ladies F.C.* She was "chaired triumphantly through the village after their first match, which was a five-to-one victory over the neighbouring village of Hooe". Commenting on some very critical letters which she received, her reaction was only to laugh them away. She said in reply, "I don't mind what people think. I like playing football and I am not going to stop it for silly people who write letters they are afraid to sign".

"THE ROYAL OAK" INN

The Royal Oak public house at Hooe was reputed to be haunted. My late mother-in-law told me that in the bedroom where they slept sometimes they thought they could hear a woman sobbing. Somebody told them that one of the past landlords was unkind to his wife, and she was very unhappy there. In the old days some of the Plymouth public houses closed earlier than the ones in the suburbs, and folk used to travel out from Plymouth and call in at *The Royal Oak* for a drink.

ABRAHAM'S GARDEN

One of the coachmen who was employed in the old Radford House once lived in Kerswell House, further up the road.

The late Mr. Tapley, who last lived at 3, Church Hill, which I think is known as *Jennycliffe Lane* now, had an interesting story to tell me about a small ridge of coastline at Jennycliffe, midway between the beach and Ramscliff Point. This spot was known as *Abraham's Garden* because while the rest of the cliff's bracken turns brown in autumn, there it remains lush and green. Mr. Tapley said he learned about the garden from his father when he was a small boy. He did not know how it got its name. A member of the Smith family who had a refreshment place on Jennycliffe, and whose family had lived in that area for sixty years, said old people of Hooe and Turnchapel said the reason the grass was always green was that old bones were underneath it. There is a theory that some Spanish slaves were sent to Plymouth at the time of the plague in 1665, and that they caught the disease and died. They were buried at Jennycliffe in Abraham's Garden. There are not many people in the village who now remember this story. Mr. Tapley said he did not remember hearing about slaves. Although there is apparently no record of this, it is recorded that at the end of the nineteenth century the Royal Naval Hospital's fever ship, *Pique*, was stationed nearby, isolating infectious disease patients, and in 1927 H.M.S. *Maud*, which belonged to the port health authorities, was there too. It has been thought that some bodies may have been deposited along the coast, and this story has been handed down.

TURNCHAPEL NAME

Turnchapel, like Oreston, has had several different names in the past. It has been known as *St. Anne's Chapel*, and *Tanchapel*. There is an old story that how it received its present name was because a contingent of soldiers was ordered to "turn by the chapel". There is probably some truth in these names, as there is an old house in Jennycliffe Lane called St. Anne's.

CAROL SINGERS

One party of carol singers on Christmas Eve was made up of Turnchapel and Oreston men, and they met outside St. Mary and All Saints Church, Plymstock. They travelled all around the parish, walking for miles, and always finished up at the *Castle Inn*, Mount Batten. There were usually two leaders, and on one occasion both arrived drunk. There were several other carol singing groups who used to go around at the same time, but most of them started from the parish church, some finishing up at the *King's Arms*, Oreston.

MR. WILLIAM HIGGINS

Two people, now both dead, of more recent years were Mr. William Higgins, a Turnchapel man, and his wife, Mrs. Ethel Louise Higgins who was formerly Miss Doddridge of Hooe. He was a naval petty officer, who survived the Battle of Jutland in the 1914–18 War, but died at the early age of fifty-two. They had one son, Tom, who was lost at sea in World War Two, and one granddaughter, who is now Mrs. Stella Treeby and lives at Oreston.

Turnchapel Branch Railway Line

This shows one of the daily passenger trains crossing the swing bridge over the entrance to Hooe Lake.

MR. AND MRS. JAMES FURSE

I feel I cannot conclude my memoirs of Hooe and Turnchapel without mentioning my late father-in-law and mother-in-law, Mr. James Furse and his wife Emily. A retired sick berth steward, R.N., he was the unofficial village doctor. They were twenty-six years in business at Hooe, first as proprietors of the *Royal Oak*, and later as first owners of what was then known as the Hooe Social Club, which Mr. Furse had built to his own design. They had two sons, James William (Bill), and Frank, the latter of which was my first husband, and they also both became sailors. Frank was a choirboy at Hooe Church before joining the Navy. He lost his life in 1940 on H.M.S. *Ardent* as also did Mr. Sidney Carder of Oreston. In memory of him, my brother-in-law, Tom, also of Hooe, and everyone else in our four villages, and elsewhere, who made the supreme sacrifice, I quote this little poem:

"Went the day well?
They died and never knew;
But well, or ill, Freedom
They died for you."

Oreston School Children

This 1920 group shows Mrs. Else Kingwell, left, and Miss Lewarn with Arthur Hendy, Kathleen Ham, Walter Spencer, Geraldine Frost, Emma Peal, Norman Carter, Edith Adams, Joyce Phillips, Doreen Kendall, Lottie Barter, Sidney Shillabeer, Ronald Pile, Prudence Smith, Edith Osborne, Jack and Fred Carder with others.

A Welsh Occasion

Dorothy Warley Pitt dresses for this occasion in the 1920s supported by Lottie Barter, Doreen Kendall, Else Richard, Kathleen Murray, Ronald Pile and Winnie Box. R. Pile was killed in action in the R.A.F. during the Second World War.

The Fields of Plymstock

These two post-war photographs clearly show the once open plan of this area when fields surrounded the village and odd houses situated around the locality. A halfway point in the development of Plymstock is recorded in these scenes which make interesting comparisons with present day ones where houses and roads criss-cross the old farming land.

Arthur L. Clamp – the man behind the books

Arthur Leslie Clamp was a man of boundless energy with a passion for helping others, particularly through his love of history. A printer by trade, he started his career in a printing company before moving his family from Exeter to Plymouth to teach at the Plymouth College of Art and Design, where he eventually became the Head of the Printing Department.

A Devoted Family Man

Arthur with his five children.

Despite his love of teaching, Arthur prioritised his family, always making it home by 5:30pm for tea. He and his wife, Rosemary, raised five children: Susan, Angela, Elizabeth, David, and Steven. Arthur would often combine his love of family and history by taking his children on Sunday walks, encouraging them to appreciate historical monuments by taking photos or making crayon rubbings of gravestones for his books. The family home at 203 Elburton Road was a hub of activity, with a large garden, featuring a two-storey fort and a makeshift swimming pool.

A Lifelong Learner and Adventurer

Arthur's thirst for knowledge extended beyond history to a deep curiosity about the world. He was passionate about exploring different cultures, traditions, and cuisines, often taking advantage of his long summer holidays as a teacher to travel to places like India, Russia, South America, the middle east and the USA, sometimes bringing one of his children along. This adventurous spirit even influenced his home life, as seen by the short-lived family tradition of steam-cooking vegetables after a trip to Iceland.

History is a prominent feature of family days out

Community and Philanthropic Spirit

His commitment to serving others was evident in his long-standing involvement with the Elburton Methodist Church. He was the Sunday School Superintendent for over 15 years and served as the editor of the wider church's monthly newsletter, "The Link," for a similar duration. After Rosemary's very sad passing, Arthur later remarried and, following a chance encounter with a professor from India, established a connection with a missionary school in Chennai. Together with his new wife, Christine, he co-founded a "Sponsor a Child's Education" program that continues to this day.

Pictured left – The cover of 'The Link' complete with hand drawn sketches of each church by Angela
Below right – Arthur Clamp promoting his latest book
Below left – Arthur at home with his first wife, Rosemary
Below centre – Arthur on holiday with his second wife, Christine

A Legacy of Learning and Positivity

Arthur's greatest passion was history, which he brought to life through tireless research, documentation, and the many books he authored. He was driven by a need to "never be stuck in a rut," constantly seeking new experiences, meeting new people, and expanding his knowledge. With a positive attitude and a great sense of humour, he was always ready to help others, leaving a lasting impact on his family and community. His children, Susan, Angela, Elizabeth, David, and Steven, remember him with love and gratitude.

David Clamp, 2025

A Legacy of Local History

Below is the story of how Arthur L Clamp began writing books, in his own words, drafted shortly before he passed away in 2001. I have only made minor alterations to this text, correcting grammatical errors that he did not survive to correct himself. When I first discovered this text, I was shocked to see my name mentioned. It seems that, unbeknownst to me, I shared my first PC with him. I suspect he used it during the day when I was at school, although I do have one memory of sitting with him and showing him how it worked. It has been a pleasure to pick up where he left off and see his books republished and redistributed, and to know that I was part of the story, even back then. It was also fascinating to discover that his pricing structure matches the way I have tried to price the books, with a third going to local sellers and the rest covering printing costs with a little left over for my expenses.

I am his eldest grandson, and it is a privilege to curate his legacy, which we are calling 'The Clamp Collection'. The very last line of the text originally reads "The following pages list all the titles." Sadly, that page is missing and we have no record of all the books he published and knowing that some of those were researched by other authors makes the process of finding them even harder. I look forward to one day completing the collection and seeing them all available again. And maybe, one day, I'll even start writing my own to add to the series. For now, here is his story in his own words.

Steven Gibson, 2025

Writing and Publishing Booklets on Local Topics and Areas

I started this interest in either 1968 or 1969 when living in Woodford. I had by these dates established the Department of Printing and I think I must have been looking for something different to do. The first titles were of A5 size proofed from type set at Clarke, Doble and Brendon, Ltd., Plymouth printers, and then made up into pages and printed at Sawtell and Neilson, Ltd., Totnes.

Then began a slow process of getting them out to shops, etc. which proved to be more time consuming and difficult than actually researching, writing and getting the books into print. However, I persisted and opened a business account with Barclays Bank on the Broadway. I was advised to give it a title so I called it "Westway Publications". There came along another problem, one of storage of paper and finished books which was solved when the family moved to Elburton in 1970.

I changed the printer to Penwell, Ltd., Callington, Cornwall, as he was then just setting up himself and his prices seemed very reasonable. I did not get any of the printers to make up the complete books. I hand folded the flat printed sheets, stitched the books on a small manual table stitcher and trimmed them in a small hand turned guillotine which I bought from someone in Penzance for £40. It was brought up in a van.

The trouble and time going to and fro to Callington was too much so I transferred the printing to PDS Printers, Prince Rock, Plymouth, and I have been with them ever since. Now they are at Plympton which is easy to reach and they fold the flat sheets which was turning out to be a long chore which only saved a small part of the printing costs.

All my first titles were written by myself. I took the photographs and developed them in the loft of the house, the type was set by now on a computer situated in the house at Elburton from which I had collected photographic lengths of text to cut up and law down as pages.

At some point I decided that I would do my own film processing of lith film so I bought a large second hand process camera from Kingsbridge and learnt through trial and error to make line negatives of the text and halftone negatives of the illustrations which proved more difficult than I anticipated. The main problem was trying to keep the developer in the large dish at the correct temperature as any change would affect the developing time. I replaced this old camera with a brand new one bought from Croydon, Surrey, costing £900. This has turned out to be a great asset cutting out an expensive part of the printer's costs and one crucial aspect of the work which I could control.

By the middle 1970s there were many outlets I had contacted in Plymouth, up to Dartmoor, Exeter, around to Torbay, Totnes, Dartmouth and the South Hams. The market for local books was much greater than I had first thought and through getting to know many local people undertaking research themselves had the chance to help and make up books for other people who had in most instances, got together a collection of photographs with some text in a rather muddled way. Through my experience in print I was able to shape up their work and get it into print and in every case I had to pay the printer and let the person have the royalties. In the majority of titles produced in this manner this was another way of producing titles and it did give some profit to my work. However, I must say that in a few cases I lost out by either the other person getting the numbers wrong, not returning any monies from stock I delivered or they thought that more of their books should have been sold.

The print run was usually 1,000 copies and from time to time I have had reprints of 250 copies. It took about ten years to clear the first print run so I always had large stocks in the garage, workshop, etc. The numbers sold during the early years was about 7,000 copies a year increasing to around 9,000 copies and for the whole of the enterprise about 500,000 have been sold. The booklets have become part of the local scene and many people collect them, shops regularly order copies and I go around certain areas month by month restocking or replacing titles as necessary.

During the past year or so I have started setting the text on a Packard Bell PC, something which I should have done some years back. I share it with Steven Gibson, my grandson. There appears to be no end to the market for local books, but I could not earn a regular income because of the long time it takes to sell stock.

However, now exceeding 100 titles made up mainly of A4 twenty-four page booklets, some folded guides, with selling prices set with a third going to the shop which is the trade custom, the original idea has been quite successful and could go on for ever.

Apart from monetary benefits, however spasmodically these might be, I have learnt a lot myself, met many interesting people and have become part of the local scene with requests to give talks and to advise people about getting into print.

Arthur L Clamp, 2001

This newspaper article, published by the Evening Herald on 17th August 2001, forms a good record of his life. Just as he encourages us to learn more about local history, we encourage you to learn a little about him. For that reason, we have included these pages at the back of all the most recently republished books, in honour of his memory and recognition of his contribution to the community.

www.ingramcontent.com/pod-product-compliance
Lightning Source LLC
Chambersburg PA
CBHW061408070526
44584CB00031B/4187